The Golden Years of
BRITISH STEAM TRAINS

Colin Garratt
on the work of
The Rev. AWV Mace

Bounty Books

First published in 1995 by Milepost Publishing
in conjunction with Arcturus Publishing Ltd,
for Bookmart Ltd.

Milepost Publishing is a division of Milepost 92 ½
Newton Harcourt,
Leicestershire LE8 9FH
Tel: 0116 2593001

Milepost 92 ½ is Colin Garratt's Audio Visual Production,
Presentation and Photographic Service for the Railway Industry.

This edition published in 2007 by Bounty Books,
a division of Octopus Publishing Group Ltd
2–4 Heron Quays, London E14 4JP
Reprinted 2009
An Hachette Livre UK Company

Text and design copyright © 1995 Milepost 92 ½
Designed by Milepost and Wilson design associates

ISBN: 978-0-753715-41-3

A CIP catalogue record for this book is available from the British Library

Printed and bound in China

INTRODUCTION

Presenting the work of the Rev. A.W.V. Mace is a joy and a privilege. Arthur Mace was born in 1908 and died in 1986; his earliest pictures date before the grouping of 1923 and he remained active as a railway photographer almost until his death. His remarkable photographic legacy, which consists of thousands of negatives embracing many sizes - both cellulose and glass plate - is now under the custodianship of Milepost 92½. The collection is being catalogued and prepared for storage in archivally safe materials.

Arthur Mace is one of a handful of individuals who have left us with a permanent vision of a past age. He was a great stylist, a great opportunist and equally at home photographing railway topography as the trains themselves.

Arthur Mace's pictures are much more than nostalgic images of a bygone age for they reveal the railway in all its dynamism in those heady days when it was the nation's principal transport system. Herein lies an essential point, for I believe that what Arthur Mace shows is the right system and that our change to a road based economy has been detrimental to the well-being of society. This book contains pictures of a viable working railway; if so magnificent a transport system could be operated with steam, how much easier it would be in today's computerised world to run an efficient modern railway fully capable of handling the nation's transport needs.

In 1939 there were 184 Dean Goods 0-6-0's in service. At the end of 1945 this total was reduced to 61, mainly through commandeering by the War Department - some being left in France after the Dunkirk evacuation. Here, we see No. 2572 heading a Pwllheli to Ruabon train on the 12th August 1935. This engine survived until 1952.

Unfortunately Arthur Mace left very few notes, either of his widespread travels or details of his pictures. In preparing this book's companion volume "The Golden Years of British Trams", which is on the work of Henry Priestley, I had the pleasure of conducting several interviews with Henry - who in common with Arthur Mace was also born in the reign of King Edward VII - and hearing at first hand the remarkable stories behind the photography. Sadly, there was no such liaison with Arthur Mace and the gap was filled by R.C. Riley, who has identified the pictures and provided background information for the captions. With a lifetime of railway experience, Dick is well suited for this task and I am grateful to him for his help.

Arthur's negatives do not easily yield their best; many are old and were taken under difficult conditions. Most of the magic is still there, but considerable expertise is needed to release it. In this respect I am heavily indebted to Glynn Wilton for fulfilling this Herculean task. Some prints took up to an hour and a half to produce, for such is Glynn's professionalism that he would never pass a print if he felt the negative could be induced to yield more.

I must also mention Helen Mace, Arthur's widow, who has herself recently been ordained to the priesthood. Without her goodwill and trust in Milepost, this book would never have been published. I hope she is pleased by this testimony to her late husband's work.

Finally to Arthur himself. Although we never met, I feel as if I knew him and even feel at times that I have been out on location with him; so communicative, so personalised, is the handwriting of his photography. Arthur used to say, tongue in cheek, that he expected to find steam trains in heaven (Isaiah Chap. 6 verse 1, mentions The Lord's train and verse 4, smoke!)

He regarded a world from which steam trains were vanishing, with dismay. Now, when the great railway age is rapidly becoming a memory, may these shining images which he left, sharpen our reflection about the best means of transport.

Colin Garratt,
Milepost 92½,
Newton Harcourt,
Leicestershire,
England.

The Golden Years of
British Steam Trains
GWR

GREAT WESTERN RAILWAY

MILEPOST

INTRODUCTION

Unlike its three rival companies, the Great Western - which dated back to the 1830s - retained its identity and absorbed a range of smaller constituent railways, principally in South Wales with such companies as the Taff Vale and Rhymney.

Locomotive development was therefore a continuous process which evolved logically throughout the nineteenth century and continued to do so until nationalisation in 1948.

Whereas the climax of motive power development occurred during the 1930s/40s in the other companies, the Great Western's final phase began at the beginning of the century with Churchward's 4-6-0 Saints and Stars. These formed a bedrock for the remainder of the company's existence and ensured a high degree of standardisation. The Saints gravitated to the Halls; the Stars to the Castles; and the Castles to the Kings.

Apart from being generic, the Great Western's locomotives were extremely handsome ; nineteenth century designs were characterised by outside frames, whilst the twentieth century ones had a very modern business like appearance. Brass chimney bands and safety valves, glorious brass number plates and name plates, green locomotives and brown and cream coaching stock endeared the railway to the general public and enthusiasts alike. It's long tradition of superb engines attracted a cult following and it was the most passionately loved of the Big Four group.

At nationalisation, the Great Western handed over 3,857 locomotives covering 60 principal classes with much of this diversity representing the tail end of the legacy inherited from the smaller absorbed railways.

Previous spread
End of the line in every sense - 0-6-0PT No. 3725 takes water at Bromyard shortly before closure in September 1964. Until 1952, the line had continued on as far as Leominster. The engine did not long outlive the branch, being withdrawn in January of 1965.

Modified Hall Class 4-6-0 No. 7905 "Fowey Hall" stands at Penzance Station with the 6.40 p.m. mail train to Paddington.

War Department Austerity 2-8-0 No. 90363 heads a freight train through the Brunel designed station at Culham between Didcot and Oxford.

King Class No. 6026 "King John" in double chimney form, stands at Shrewsbury with the Cambrian Coast Express from Paddington. The train will be worked forward from this point by smaller engines.

Hawksworth 0-6-0PT No. 8487 stands at the buffer stops of Paddington's platform 1 having brought empty stock from Old Oak Common for a down express.

Busy scene at Birmingham Snow Hill as 4-6-0 No. 6854 "Roundhill Grange" enters on an up excursion. Sadly, this fine station was closed and demolished in 1972 and only in recent years has a small substitute appeared for local services.

Bound for Ruabon and the Midlands, 2-6-0 No. 6311 crosses the Mawddach Estuary on the approach to Barmouth Junction having followed the coast from Dovey Junction to Morfa Mawddach.

Opposite
1400 Class 0-4-2T No. 5811 bowls a two coach train along the scenic branch from Bala to Blaenau Festiniog.

Tyseley based 0-6-0PT No. 3625 emerges from the stygian gloom of the tunnel and runs light into Birmingham Snow Hill Station.

Another light engine movement in the form of 0-6-0PT No. 4671 caught standing at Severn Tunnel Junction Station.

The Castle Class 4-6-0's were overwhelmingly named after castles although some earls, a few notable people and famous aircraft of the R.A.F. were also commemorated as in this picture showing Reading based No. 5076 "Gladiator".

Previous spread
The Mayflower - 8.30 a.m. Plymouth to Paddington - made its first stop at Exeter St. David's where it is seen arriving behind a King Class 4-6-0.

Severn Tunnel based Churchward 2-8-0 No. 2826 drifts slowly beside bridge engineering works.

On a wet day at Shrewsbury No. 7823 "Hook Norton Manor" heads the down Cambrian Coast Express.

A double chimney King leaves Paddington in December 1962 with a down express for Wolverhampton.

Previous spread
William Dean's Barnum Class 2-4-0s were introduced on to the Great Western in 1889. They had sandwich frames and were extremely successful engines. Here we see No. 3223 preparing to turn at Gresty Lane, having worked into Crewe from Wellington. This example survived until 1936, the class becoming extinct the following year.

A Hawksworth County Class 4-6-0 makes a business like departure from Penzance with the up Cornishman.

Tyseley based 0-6-2T No. 5647 heads a West Midlands freight train. Two hundred of these freight hauling tanks were built between 1924 and 1928 primarily for service throughout the vast coalfields of South Wales.

Opposite page
A Churchward Class 43XX, 2-6-0 heads the Hastings to Birkenhead through train amid the outer suburbs of Birmingham.

One of the popular Saint Class 4-6-0's No. 2924 "St. Helena" enters Exeter St. David's with a north to west express, the formation including two ex-L.N.W.R. carriages. Built in 1907, No. 2924 lasted until 1950.

Duke Class 4-4-0 No. 3252 "Duke of Cornwall" stands in Shrewsbury Station in April 1935. Built in 1895 it was withdrawn in 1937 being replaced by a Dukedog 4-4-0.

Castle Class 4-6-0 No. 4095 "Harlech Castle" of Plymouth Laira Shed, stands in Bristol Temple Meads Station with an up empty stock train.

Churchward Class 43XX, 2-6-0 No. 7305 of Banbury Shed, stands at Leamington Spa General on a down stopping passenger train in August 1960. The camera wielding enthusiast seems totally absorbed in the proceedings.

A double chimneyed Castle Class 4-6-0 on arrival at Paddington with the tightly timed Bristolian express. During the summer of 1959 this train was scheduled to cover the 118 miles between Paddington and Bristol in 100 minutes.

Opposite page
Another double chimneyed Castle at Worcester Shrub Hill on the up Cathedrals Express to Paddington.

0-6-0ST No. 1331 was a former Whitland and Cardigan Railway engine taken over by the Great Western in 1886. Built by Fox Walker & Co. in 1877, it was re-built at Swindon in 1927 and after a spell working on the Weymouth Harbour Tramway, it was transferred to Oswestry where this picture was made. The veteran was finally withdrawn in 1950.

1076 Class double framed 0-6-0PT No. 1574 was built as an 0-6-0ST in 1879 and rebuilt to the form seen here in 1927. Caught shunting at Oxford, No. 1574 was one of the last survivors of this large class and remained in service until 1937. Note the typical G.W.R. shunter's truck.

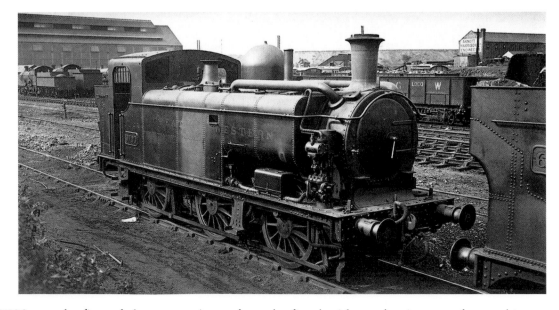

0-6-0PT No. 9700 was the first of eleven pannier tanks to be fitted with condensing gear for working over Metropolitan Railway sub-surface lines to the G.W.R. depot at Smithfield. The engine is seen at Old Oak Common Shed.

Ex-M.&S.W.J.R. 2-4-0 No. 1334 at Didcot on 11th May 1936. No. 1334 was one of three engines built by Dubs & Co. in 1894 and fitted with a G.W.R. standard boiler in 1924. These engines were used on the branch from Newbury to Lambourne.

Another double framed 0-6-0PT No. 1565 at Didcot, also on 11th May 1936. This example is fitted with a spark arresting chimney for working in local military stores depots. It survived until 1938.

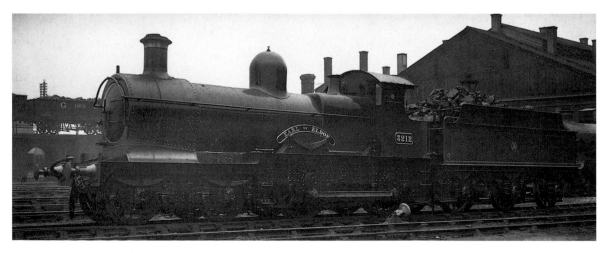

The Dukedogs were a hybrid of Duke type boilers on Bulldog frames. These lively 4-4-0 s were light enough to work on lines such as those in the Cambrian section over which many larger engines were forbidden. No. 3212 "Earl of Eldon" is seen new at Swindon in May 1937. This engine was only named for a few weeks as its nameplates were transferred to the Castle Class 4-6-0 No. 5055 in July 1937.

Class 14XX, 0-4-2T No. 1401 stands in the bay of the decrepit looking Banbury Station which was to be re-built in B.R. days. No. 1401 was in charge of a push and pull train to Chipping Norton and Kingham.

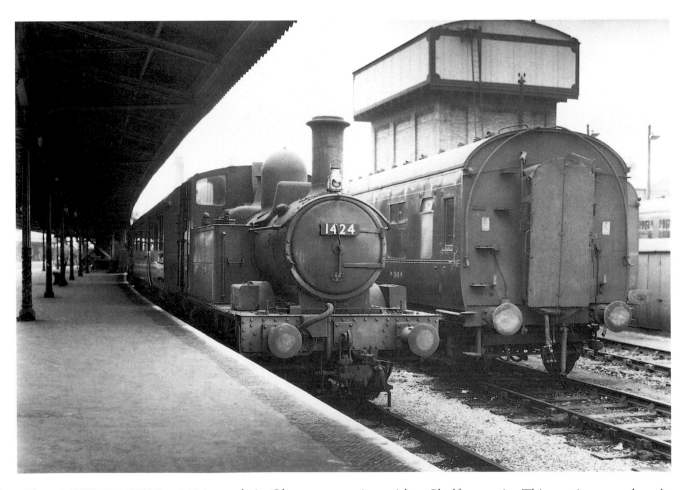

Another Class 14XX, 0-4-2T No. 1424 stands in Gloucester station with a Chalfont train. This service ceased at the end of 1964 and was the last push and pull working on former G.W.R. lines.

The happy days of the School Treat are beautifully captured here by Arthur Mace. Invariably the excursions would be by train and performing the honours on this occasion is an 0-6-0PT.

Previous spread
Birmingham Snow Hill was one of Britain's best loved stations. It's architecture, it's light and shade effects, it's bustling atmosphere and glorious diversity of trains endeared it to the nation. Much of the magic is caught here as a King Class 4-6-0 arrives on a Birkenhead to Paddington express.

Churchward's first 2-8-0 was built in 1903 and by 1919 there were 84 in service. Remarkably, between 1938 and 1942, a further 83 similar engines were built. No. 3842, seen on an unfitted freight train, was one of the later built engines.

Wolverhampton Oxley based 0-6-0PT No. 9630 marshalling a freight train. Note the G.W.R. Toad brake van behind the engine.

Oxford based Hall Class 4-6-0 No. 6956 "Mottram Hall" approaches the outskirts of Birmingham with a down inter regional express.

Modified Hall No. 6992 "Arborfield Hall" enters Worcester Shrub Hill with an up Hereford express.

Previous spread
Castle Class 4-6-0 No. 5046 "Earl Cawdor" enters Shrewsbury with a down train during the early 1960 s.

On 27th April 1963 the semi-final of the F.A. cup was played at Aston Villa's ground. It brought 15 special trains from the Southampton area to Birmingham Snow Hill, all but one being hauled by Bulleid light Pacific's. Three of the football specials went via Worcester and were piloted by Class 8F 2-8-0's from Stourbridge. One of these, No. 48478, has assisted No. 34009 "Lyme Regis" on the 07.10 a.m. from Southampton. As the supporters leave Snow Hill Station the fireman stands in the Pacific's tender shovelling coal forward.

It's thumbs up from the train spotters eagerly awaiting the specials as No. 34088 "213 Squadron" heads the 08.49a.m. from Southampton Central into Birmingham Snow Hill.

Un-rebuilt Bulleid Pacific No. 34094 "Mortehoe" enters Birmingham Snow Hill with the 08.00 a.m. special from Southampton Central.

This delightful veteran was built by Sharp Stewart of Manchester in 1866. Numbered 1197, she was one of three 2-4-0Ts constructed for the Cambrian Railways and is seen in Oswestry Shed. She survived until 1948.

Three of the six 1934 built 1366 Class 0-6-0PTs in the stock shed at Swindon. Their main use was shunting those sidings in the works that required short wheel base engines and also on the Weymouth Harbour Tramway. In their final years they replaced the veteran Beattie 2-4-0Ts at Wadebridge for the line to Wenford Bridge.

At Towyn on the Cambrian Coast Line, the 2' 3" gauge Talyllyn Railway is within easy access of the G.W.R. station. Talyllyn Railway 0-4-0WT "Dolgoch" of 1866 vintage stands at the line's Abergnolwyn terminus.

Castle Class 4-6-0 No.5046 "Earl Cawdor" - a Wolverhampton Stafford Road engine - has arrived at Shrewsbury

Dukedog 4-4-0 No. 9017 and a highly polished Manor 4-6-0 stand in Shrewsbury Station having been rostered to work the Cambrian Coast Express.

Castle Class 4-6-0 No. 4078 "Pembroke Castle" in the up centre road at Bristol Temple Meads with two coaches to be added to the formation of an up Weston Super Mare express.

At the buffer stops at platform 1 Paddington where Hawksworth 0-6-0PT No. 9415 has brought in the empty coaches for the 11.30 a.m. Penzance departure. These were one of the last Great Western designs to be built; they were ordered at the end of 1947, immediately before nationalisation, and building continued into the early 1950's.

An Oswestry based Dean goods 0-6-0 No. 2424, heads a stopping passenger train. This engine escaped military service and was withdrawn in 1946.

The famous Bulldogs were introduced in 1898. They had a wonderful variety of names ranging from places in the British Empire, birds, notable rivers and famous celebrities. Most of the nameplates were of the traditional crescent design fitted to the forward wheel splashers but the example seen here is one of a few provided with oval cabside plates bearing both the name and the engine's number. The engine is No. 3327 "Marco Polo" caught at Chester in April 1935 and withdrawn the following year. No. 3327 was one of the Bulldogs with curved frames; straight frames were introduced on the class commencing with No. 3341 in 1900.

Aberdare Class 2-6-0 No. 2676 running light near Oxford in 1935. These classic Dean engines were introduced in 1900 initially for work around the South Wales coalfields, hence their name. The type was given an extended life owing to World War Two and No. 2676 was not withdrawn until 1946; the last survivor following three years later

At Paddington, Oxford's No. 4979 "Wooton Hall" provides unusual motive power for the down Cathedrals Express normally worked by a Worcester Castle.

No. 6853 "Morehampton Grange" stands on an up express in the up loop platform at Birmingham's Snow Hill.

Castle Class 4-6-0 No. 7031 "Cromwell's Castle" stands on the down relief line at Reading General at the head of a down Worcester express.

Previous spread
Another golden moment from the football specials on 27th April 1963 when the semi final of the F.A. cup was played at Aston Villa's ground bringing 15 special trains from the Southampton area into Birmingham Snow Hill. Here, entering Snow Hill's up platform is Stanier 8F No. 48417 piloting No. 34039 "Boscastle" on the 07.43 a.m. from Southampton. In the down platform stands No. 34094, one of only two un-rebuilt Bullied Pacifics used on these specials.

Appropriately named Hawksworth 4-6-0 No. 1006 "County of Cornwall" stands in Penzance Station with an up express.

Castle Class 4-6-0 No.5089 "Westminster Abbey" pauses in Bristol Temple Meads with the up Cornishman 10.30 am Penzance to Wolverhampton. Note the bevy of train spotters immersed in their task.

At Birmingham Snow Hill, No.5955 "Garth Hall" of Didcot pauses with a down stopping train.

Previous spread
Crossing the River Dee at Chester, Class 5700 0-6-0PT No. 8730 heads an empty wagon train towards Saltney. These humble engines constituted Britain's largest class totalling 863 engines built between 1929 and 1949.

A Class 1400 0-4-2T propels a B.R. built railmotor trailer on the approach to Hightown with a Wrexham to Ellesmere service.

Another push and pull train, probably on a Stourbridge service, with a Class 6400, 0-6-0PT in charge. The railmotor trailers are of G.W.R. and B.R. design respectively whilst behind the engine is a former L.M.S. van and a covered goods wagon.

The Golden Years of
British Steam Trains
LMS

LONDON MIDLAND & SCOTTISH RAILWAY

MILEPOST

INTRODUCTION

The L.M.S. was the largest of the Big Four companies with territory ranging from Bristol to the Highlands of Scotland. Over ten thousand locomotives were inherited in 1923 from some of the largest railway companies in Britain such as the London and North Western, The Midland and the Caledonian. The L.M.S. was a rich potpourri of locomotive design and an extremely innovative railway especially during the tenancy of William Stanier who was Chief Mechanical Engineer from 1932 to 1944.

The Stanier years were one of the most productive periods in British railway history and produced a magnificent range of designs which revolutionised the L.M.S.'s motive power. The 8F 2-8-0 and Black Five 4-6-0s which together totalled over 1,700 engines, rapidly heralded the withdrawal of dozens of outmoded classes. Designs by Stanier and his successors Charles Fairburn and H.G. Ivatt, formed the basis for some of British Railways' standard designs built from 1951 onwards. When the L.M.S. passed into British Railways in 1948, it possesed 7,850 locomotives embracing 100 different designs.

Former LMS compound No. 41162 was a Rugby based engine. She was built by the Vulcan Foundry in 1925 and was one of the last survivors of the Compound 4-4-0 s. She was withdrawn in 1960 and the class became extinct the following year.

Ex-LNWR George V Class 4-4-0 No. 25348 "Coronation" at speed with express passenger headlights. "Coronation" was the 5,000th engine built at Crewe works. She was withdrawn in 1940 after a working life of only 29 years. A preservation attempt was made and the engine languished in store for some years before tragically being broken up. The engine's name was duplicated in 1938 by the first of Stanier's Coronation Pacific's.

Previous spread
Webb built eight 0-4-2ST Crane Engines between 1892 and 1895 for duties at Crewe and Wolverton works. As service locomotives they retained their LNWR numbers in LMS days. No.3249, seen here at Crewe freshly out-shopped, was one of the last two survivors being withdrawn in 1947.

Several London and North Western Railway Claughton 4-6-0s were modified for the Midland Division loading gauge. No. 6005 is seen coupled to a tender from a Great Central design R.O.D. 2-8-0. This engine was replaced in 1932 by a Patriot Class 4-6-0 which eventually became No. 5509. On the left is 1867 built Midland Railway 2-4-0 No. 8, which survived until 1942.

Hughes Crab 2-6-0 No. 42886 and Stanier Class 5, 4-6-0 No. 44747 stand at Manchester Victoria.

This wonderful picture was one of Arthur Mace's favourites. He called it "A Crimson Rambler on it's native heath". Taken at 11am on a sunny July day in 1928, it shows a Midland Compound piloting a Deeley Belpaire 4-4-0 at Derby, the Midland Railway's spiritual home. In the background is a London and North Western Prince of Wales 4-6-0 on a Nottingham to Llandudno express.

Arthur Mace regularly visited Euston Station over a 35 year period and made a series of pictures of trains at the buffer stops. This scene, taken shortly after the grouping, shows a London and North Western Jumbo 2-4-0 acting as pilot to a Prince of Wales Class 4-6-0.

Ex-LNWR 0-6-2T Coal Tank No. 58900 (formally LMS 7699). This well known engine brought a latter day touch of North Western styling to Birmingham New Street where it ended its days as station pilot during the early 1950s working from Monument Lane shed. It was finally withdrawn in 1954.

Opposite
Ex-S&DJR Class 2P 4-4-0, No. 40634 stands at the buffer stops at Bath Green Park having assisted a BR Class 9F 2-10-0 over the Mendip Hills from Evercreech Junction with an express from Bournemouth West to the north.

This is one of Arthur Mace's finest pictures and shows an unidentified rebuilt Claughton 4-6-0 heading a mixed freight. Believed to be a pre-war scene, the engine is possibly the last survivor No. 6004 (formally Princess Louise). The once 130 strong Claughton Class was an epic design in locomotive history and when No. 6004 was withdrawn in 1949 the London & North Western express passenger dynasty passed to extinction.

An ex-London & North Western Precursor 4-4-0 carries out a strange shunting movement in North Wales.

Former London & North Western Prince of Wales Class 4-6-0 No. 25704 "Scotia" heads a stopping passenger train.

Previous spread
Still in Midland Railway livery, Deeley 0-6-4T No. 2004 acts as Derby Station pilot with the works in the background. Known as Flatirons these engines were intended to replace Johnson's 0-4-4Ts on passenger work, but due to a tendency to derail they were confined to freight working. One of the Midland Railway's few unhappy designs, all had disappeared by 1938.

Over page
Ex-LNWR 2-4-2 No. 46757 is seen here in charge of a Stephenson Locomotive Society special which ran over closed branches in the Birmingham area on 3rd June in 1950. Based at Walsall, this 1897 built veteran survived until 1953. One hundred and sixty of these engines were built during the 1890s for branch and cross country work on the former London & North Western system; all had gone by 1955.

A pair of Class 3F Jinty 0-6-0Ts stand as shunting pilots at Crewe bringing a latter day Midland flavour to the heart of the former London & North Western empire.

Crewe based Stanier Pacific No. 46251 "City of Nottingham" stands on the arrival side of the old Euston before that station's drastic re-build.

Re-built Patriot Class 4-6-0 No. 45527 "Southport" heads through Crewe en-route to Liverpool with a Cunard special. The last Cunard sailing from Liverpool took place in 1966.

A Jubilee 4-6-0 approaches Bromsgrove Station having descended the famous 1 in 37 Lickey Incline.

Ex-Midland Railway Class 4F 0-6-0 No. 43940 heads a southbound freight at Evesham. The former Great Western station can just be glimpsed on the far right.

Ex-London & North Western 0-8-0 No. 8942 freshly out-shopped from Crewe works after a major overhaul, is "run in" on light duty. Despite the introduction of some 700 Stanier 8Fs, these classic London & North Western heavy haulers remained ubiquitous well into the 1950's.

This incident at Stafford would have appealed to Arthur Mace's sense of humour. It shows LMS Class 3F Jinty 0-6-0T No. 47649 which has got itself into trouble while shunting a ventilated fruit van.

With the banking engine already attached, a Jubilee Class 4-6-0 takes water prior to ascending the Lickey Incline,
meanwhile a Great Western Hall Class 4-6-0 waits with a freight train.

Previous page
Royal Scot Class 4-6-0 No. 46168 "The Girl Guide" surmounts the summit of the Lickey Incline at Blackwell with a
lightweight three coach stopping passenger train. The Lickey Incline is Britain's steepest main line gradient.

Towards the end of steam, many locomotives lost their smokebox numberplates as with this Fairburn 2-6-4T standing in Bradford Exchange with a train bound for Leeds City.

Jubilee Class 4-6-0 No. 45576 "Bombay" stands at the buffer stops at number 7 platform in St. Pancras with an arrival from Sheffield. To the delight of train spotters, this engine - along with other Jubilee's named after Indian states - formed part of a transfer from the Scottish Region to the Midland Division in exchange for a batch of long serving Midland Jubilee's.

Stanier Class 5, 4-6-0 No. 45431 heads a special train through Beverley Yorks. This engine was one of the last survivors of the once 842 strong Black 5's and lasted almost until the end of steam, finally being withdrawn in 1967.

LMS designed Ivatt 2-6-2T No.41299 takes a breather from working empty stock trains at London's Cannon Street Station. Having taken this picture at 5pm on the 13th July 1954, Arthur Mace "lost" the film. It was found almost 16 years later on the 20th June 1970 and processed immediately with the happy result shown here which says a lot for the keeping qualities of Ilford FPS.

Hughes "Crab" 2-6-0s were seldom seen working passenger trains on the southern reaches of the Midland Main Line. Occasionally however, they would turn up on specials like this one heading southwards through Market Harborough.

The magic that was once Warrington Bank Quay Station; a Patriot 4-6-0 heads an up express; a Stanier Class 8F 2-8-0 awaits the road whilst Ivatt 2-6-2T No. 41211 performs on the Earlestown push and pull train.

Two unidentified Prince of Wales Class 4-6-0s. The leading engine is one of five fitted with Walschaerts valve gear in 1923/4. This picture is taken from one of Arthur Mace's 35mm negatives, a format he partially adopted in the post war years. The definition compares well with the much larger formats and glass plates of his pre-war work.

Over page
The first LMS Stanier Pacific No. 6200 "The Princess Royal" stands at Euston, a brand new engine in 1933. The Camden shed code 1 was changed to 1B in 1935. The original flat sided tender as applied to the first two members of this class looks incongruous and was soon replaced with the later standard variety.

Ex-MR Class 3F Jinty 0-6-0T No. 47249 undergoing a general overhaul in Derby Works in early BR days.

Possibly on the same visit to Derby Works, Arthur Mace found the cylinders of a Midland Compound 4-4-0. The low pressure ones with a diameter of 21 inches are placed at either side whilst the high pressure one of 19 inches diameter is at the centre.

A line-up of preserved engines in the paint shop at Crewe Works. From left to right, LNWR 2-4-0 No. 790 "Hardwicke"; 2-2-2 No. 3020 "Cornwall"; the Furness Railway 0-4-0 "Coppernob"; the replica of Stephenson's "Rocket" and 18 inch gauge 0-4-0T "Pet". Both Crewe and Horwich Works had extensive 18 inch gauge internal systems on which similar engines were employed for moving components and materials around the works site.

Over Page
With steam drifting helpfully for Arthur Mace, Stanier 8F 2-8-0 No. 48295 heads an up-freight through Stafford. The train spotters perched on top of the wall complete this early 1950's scene when steam trains were going to last forever.

Ex-L&YR 4-6-0 No. 10415 in London & North Western livery stands at the buffer stops at Liverpool Exchange. Note the sign directing passengers to race trains for Aintree.

A traditional line-up amid the interior of the Midland Railway roundhouse at Saltley, Birmingham with Class 3F 0-6-0s, 43435, 43674, 43680, 43620 and Class 4F 0-6-0, 43949.

Rendered surplus on the LT&SR lines by Stanier 3 cylinder 2-6-4Ts, this "Intermediate" Tilbury 4-4-2T of Class 2P No. 2104 has found its way to Mansfield for use on Nottingham trains. Other Tilbury 4-4-2s gravitated to Toton, Leicester and Skipton and the four examples from this last mentioned location ended their days rotting at Carlisle Durran Hill.

Arthur Mace remained active photographing steam until its final demise in 1968. During steam's final years he was resident in Birmingham and did many scenes in the area like this study of Black 5 No. 45058 in begrimed condition ekeing out its final days.

Ivatt Mogul 2-6-0, No. 46492 was one of a class of 128 engines built between 1946 and 1952. These useful light, mixed traffic engines then formed the basis for British Railways Standard 78000 Class.

British Railways Standard Britannia Pacific No. 70046 "Anzac" at Sutton Coldfield in 1962 during it's brief sojourn at Aston depot. Shortly after this picture was taken, the engine returned to it's former home depot at Holyhead. "Anzac" was withdrawn in July 1967 and broken up by Campbell's at Airdrie in January 1968.

Ex-North London Railway's 0-6-0T No. 27514. Although several were transferred to the Crompton and High Peak line based on Rowsley, this engine remained on its native territory at Devons Road Bow.

Another service locomotive to retain its London & North Western number, if not its number plate, was 0-6-0T No. 3323 used as a Crewe Works shunter. This much sought after veteran of the LNWR survived on internal duties at Crewe Works until 1954.

Another Crewe Works shunter of the same period was LNWR Coal Engine, 0-6-0 No. 8245 built in 1889. Not officially regarded as service stock, the engine acquired its BR number 58347. This engine, along with several sisters, survived on internal duties at Crewe long after other members of the class had been withdrawn finally disappearing in 1953.

Crewe Works also employed LNWR special tank number 27334 "Liverpool". This 1867 built engine survived until 1939.

An ex-works repaint at Crewe for Class G2A 0-8-0 number 48899. Built as a Webb Compound in 1904, she was converted to simple expansion 3 years later and was finally re-built with Belpaire boiler in 1941.

The evacuation special of Dulwich College Prep School to Betsycoed from West Dulwich in 1942. The L.N.W.R. Coal Tank seen here would have taken over at Llandudno Jnc. 1995 was the 50th Anniversary of the boys return to Dulwich.

Previous spread
Shrewsbury based Ivatt Class 2, 2-6-2T No. 41203 is the subject of much interest from the local train spotters as it stands at the lengthy platform at Kidderminster with a Severn Valley Line train.

This London and North Western scene at Shrewsbury is another of Arthur Mace's North Wales classics. On the left is an ex-L.N.W.R. Webb 2-4-2T seen with one of that designer's slightly earlier 0-6-2T Coal Tanks.

One of Webb's ubiquitous London and North Western Coal Tank 0-6-2Ts which formed a class of 300 locomotives built between 1881 and 1896. Once prolific across the vast London and North Western territories, most of the last survivors ended their days in Wales working two or three coach branch line trains as depicted here at an unknown location. All survivors had gone by 1958.

An exhibition of locomotives and rolling stock was held at Euston in 1938 to commemorate the centenary of the London and Birmingham Railway. This prestigious line-up is led by Liverpool and Manchester Railway 0-4-2 "Lion" of 1838; Princess Coronation Class 4-6-2 No. 6225 "Duchess of Gloucester" of 1938; George V Class 4-4-0 No. 25348 "Coronation" of 1911 and 2-2-2 "Cornwall" of 1847.

At the British Empire Exhibition at Wembley in 1924, ex-LNWR, 2-2-2 "Columbine" was dwarfed by LMS No. 11114, a 4-6-4T of L&YR design built in that year.

A former L&NWR 4-4-0 heads an express passenger train round the curve into Chester.

Previous spread
Another scene taken from one of Arthur Mace's post war 35mm negatives reveals ex-LNWR Prince of Wales Class 4-6-0 No. 25673 "Lusitania". This engine was one of the last two Prince of Wales to remain in service being withdrawn in 1949. The generic LNWR family likeness with the 0-8-0 in the background is unmistakable.

Over page
Hughes 4-6-0 No. 10452 built by the LMS to L&YR design stands in Crewe Station at the head of an express for Carlisle. After a remarkably short working life, this engine was withdrawn in 1936.

An ex-L&YR 4-4-2 "High Flyer" Atlantic shunting empty stock. Forty of these fast running engines were built between 1899 and 1902, the last one being withdrawn in 1934.

Arthur Mace's station scenes represent some of his most exciting work. Some are topographical, others feature people very prominently as in this one revealing a parade of light engines passing through Rugby led by Nuneaton based Hughes Crab 2-6-0 No. 42888.

LNWR George V Class 4-4-0 No. 25376 "Snipe", a Chester engine, stands on an express passenger train.

The introduction of Stanier's designs during the 1930's led to either the withdrawal of former LNW express passenger designs or their relegation to secondary work as in this instance of Bletchley based 4-6-0 No. 25673 "Lusitania" ekeing out her final days in the post war period with a stopping passenger train.

Previous spread
Ex-L&YR 2-4-2T No. 10872 allocated to Agecroft shed Salford, heads a local passenger train at Manchester Victoria while a near relative in the form of L&YR 0-6-0 No. 52300 stands on a parcels train.

The Golden Years of
British Steam Trains
LNER

LONDON & NORTH EASTERN RAILWAY

MILEPOST

INTRODUCTION

The L.N.E.R was the second largest of the Big Four companies. It inherited a remarkable range of locomotives from such major pre-grouping companies as the Great Northern, Great Eastern, Great Central, North Eastern and North British. It's territory ranged from London and East Anglia to Aberdeen and beyond. Rivalry with the L.M.S. for services between London and Scotland was legendary and dated back to the exciting railway races of 1888 and 1895 which were performed by the coordinated efforts of major railway companies on either side of Britain.

The L.N.E.R.'s locomotive giant was Nigel Gresley, who took over as Chief Mechanical Engineer from the outset having previously held that position on the Great Northern Railway. Gresley's big designs are amongst the most famous in railway history, especially his A3 and A4 Pacifics whilst lesser known designs, like his mighty P1/P2 2-8-2s of 1925, were equally awe inspiring.

The L.N.E.R. did not pursue locomotive standardisation so vigorously as the other companies and it was not until Edward Thompson took over as chief Mechanical Engineer in 1941 that the B1 mixed traffic 4-6-0s were introduced and rapidly decimated a vast array of older types. In spite of this, nationalisation saw the L.N.E.R. hand over to British Railways an incredible 150 different classes totalling 6,550 locomotives.

Profile of a Class N2, 0-6-2T No.69498, having brought in empty stock to Kings Cross terminus.

Opposite
A pair of Thompson engines caught in begrimed condition towards the end of steam. On the left is Class L1, 2-6-4T No.67740 with a B1 Class 4-6-0.

Previous spread
A wartime view at the north end of York Station. Class A4, 4-6-2 No.4499, "Sir Murrough Wilson" on a northbound train while a grimy Class V2, 2-6-2 heads south.

M.&G.N. 4-4-0 No.80 in charge of a heavy train near Sheringham. Of Midland Railway Johnson design, it was among the stock of M.&G.N. engines taken over by the L.N.E.R. in 1936 but was soon withdrawn.

A typically Derby designed 4-4-0 No.54 of the M.&G.N. heads an express near Sheringham. It survived only three years after the 1936 L.N.E.R. take-over.

On the L.M.S, this engine would have been a Class 3F 0-6-0, but on the M.&G.N. No.62 was to become L.N.E.R. Class D41 in 1936. Unlike its L.M.S. counterparts, this engine also suffered an early withdrawal in 1939.

L.N.E.R. Class A8, 4-6-2T No.9851 at Newcastle. These engines originally comprised a class of 45 4-4-4Ts built for the
North Eastern Railway between 1913 and 1922. All were re-built to 4-6-2T's during the 1930's.

Over page
A sad state for one of the graceful Great Central Railway Class C4, 4-4-2s known as Jersey Lilies. The engine is seen here
receiving attention on the sheerlegs at Woodford shortly before her withdrawal in the late 1940's.

Ex-Great Central Railway Class N5 0-6-2T No.9352, and Class C13, 4-4-2T No.67417 stand on local trains in the Cheshire Lines Committee terminus at Chester Northgate.

The symmetry of a 4-4-4T was a joy to behold and here North Eastern Railway Class H1, No.2147 is in her original form at York prior to being re-built as a 4-6-2T. She survived in re-built form as No.69854 until 1960.

A post war view of Class A4 Pacific No.60009 "Union of South Africa" entering Newcastle on the Flying Scotsman.

Durham Station in L.N.E.R. days with a V2, 2-6-2 on the left and an A3 Pacific.

One of Arthur Mace's most exciting pictures and dated 1946/7. The Gresley V2, 2-6-2 has drawn well up in the platform and threatens to obscure the view of the A4 Pacific approaching at speed much to the chagrin of the train spotters who are in a clear state of emotional agitation.

The up Flying Scotsman approaches York behind the record breaking Class A3 Pacific No.2750 "Papyrus".

An A1 Pacific speeds through Durham with an up express.

Over page
At Kings Cross shed Class J52, 0-6-0T No.4213 stands beside a large boilered Ivatt Atlantic. Unusually for a London based engine, the J52 is not fitted with condensing gear. As No.68800 it was withdrawn in 1958.

Cambridge engines started working one through train over the former London & North Western line to Oxford in 1954.
Here, Class D16/3, 4-4-0 No.62585 leaves Oxford on the return journey.

Opposite
In un-rebuilt form with A.C.F.I. feed water heater, Class B12, 4-6-0 No.8569 heads a Kings Cross buffet car express. It was
re-built as Class B12/3 in 1933 and, as No.61569 was withdrawn in 1957.

Later in 1938, the Stirling Single ran a special to and from Cambridge with the old stock. This was organised by the R.C.T.S.

No.1 backs on to its train at Kings Cross with admiring glances from all occupants of the platform along with the crew of Class N2, 0-6-2T No.4766.

Opposite
Prior to the 1938 acceleration of the Flying Scotsman, a replica of the 1888 train of seven 6 wheeled coaches was hauled by the preserved Stirling Single 4-2-2 No.1 which was specially brought out of the old York museum and overhauled. It ran from Kings Cross as far as Stevenage, where guests transferred to the new train.

Thompson Class L1 2-6-4T No.67758 of Neasden, hauls a train of ex-L.M.S. non corridor stock through the outer suburbs of London.

Gorton based Thompson B1 Class No.61265 at the head of an excursion composed of ex-L.M.S. corridor stock. Between 1942 and 1950, 410 of these general purpose engines were built.

935 of these Austerity 2-8-0s were built for the War Department during World War Two. After service abroad, most returned to B.R. and here No.90582 of Mexborough is seen hauling a freight on the Great Central Main Line. No British locomotives were as neglected as these Austerities. They were always filthy with cabside numbers indicipherable. They could be heard approaching over long distances by the heavy 'plonk' of banging bushes. An Austerity version of Stanier's L.M.S. 8F 2-8-0 they lacked any family lineage and were stark austere machines. They had few devotees and yet were one of the most exciting classes for trainspotters as 773 of them roamed Britain working from dozens of different sheds. Their tasks often involved inter colliery transfers and they had the delightful habit of turning up miles off their home territory.

Ex-G.N.R. J6 Class 0-6-0 No.64267 was one of the last survivors of its class and was allocated to Colwick Depot, Nottingham.

Ex-North British Railway Class D34, 4-4-0 No.2426 "Cuddie Headrigg" of Perth heads a local passenger train.

Arthur Mace has caught the essence of a country branch line with this scene at the terminus of the Easingwold Railway which ran for some two miles from Alne on the East Coast Main Line. In 1947, the railway's Hudswell Clark, 0-6-0T needed extensive repair and a class J71 or J72 was hired from York. Here, Class J71 0-6-0T No.68246 stands with the railway's ex-G.C.R. coach. The line closed in 1957.

Heading for Liverpool Street, Class N7 0-6-2T No.2615 leaves Stratford with a train of G.E.R. suburban stock.

Ex-N.B.R Class C15, 4-4-2T No.67460 pauses on the Caigendoran-Arrochar and Tarbet push and pull service.

Manning Wardle built 0-4-2T No.8192 of Class Z5, one of two built for use at Aberdeen docks. It was withdrawn in 1960.

Both these engines were based at Kittybrewster with two similar engines of Class Z4. No.8193, also seen at Aberdeen, was withdrawn in 1956.

Ex-North British Railway Class J88, 0-6-0T No.9235 of 1909, shunts at Leith docks. As B.R. No.68334 the engine survived until 1959. Introduced by Reid, these dock tanks with 3' 9" diameter wheels were built between 1915/1919. All had vanished by 1962.

Over page
Ivatt large boilered Atlantic Class C1, 4-4-2 No.4427 heads a stopping passenger train near Cambridge. These large boilered engines, introduced in 1902 revolutionised express passenger services on the Great Northern and much publicity was made about the girth of their boilers. When Nigel Gresley succeeded Henry Ivatt as Chief Mechanical Engineer of the Great Northern Railway, he modified the engines with high degree superheating which made their performance even more dynamic and on many occasions they deputised sucessfully for Pacifics on the heavy Anglo Scottish expresses. The first of these engines was withdrawn in 1943 and, literally worn out from years of hard work, the remainder followed, the last one disappearing in 1950.

Former North Eastern Railway 4-6-0 No.929 of Class B16 at York Station. Built in 1921, this handsome engine was withdrawn as No.61424 in 1960.

Ex-North British Railway 0-6-0 No.5267 was built at Cowlairs in 1892. She belonged to Class J36 which consisted of 168 engines.

Ex-North British Railway 4-4-0 No.62485 "Glen Murran" of Class D34 pauses with a train at Edinburgh Waverley.

Hull based War Department Austerity 2-8-0 No.90688 passes through Beverley Road with a freight train.

The end of the road - Gresley Class N2, 0-6-2T No's.69557 and 69566 on the scrap line at Doncaster works. Built in 1925, they were withdrawn in 1957.

The boiler shop at Doncaster works.

Another scene at Doncaster works, this one in the Erecting Shop where one of the later built K3, Class 2-6-0s No.61959 of 1936 vintage awaits a light repair. At the time this picture was taken, No. 61959 was allocated to Lowestoft.

Previous spread
A G.C.R. 2-8-0 of class 04 heads a fitted freight train of perishables. This class was built in large numbers for use overseas in World War I.

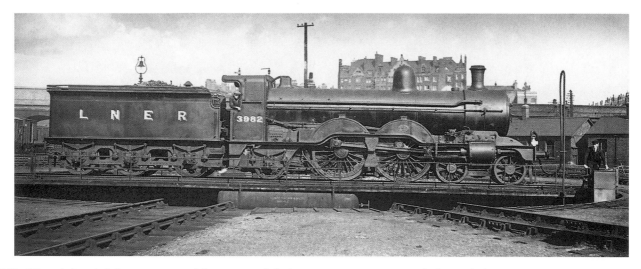

The G.N.R. Klondyke 4-4-2s - so named because of their emergence in 1897 followed the great Gold Rush to the Yukon - were the first Atlantics in Britain. Only twenty two were built and they were soon eclipsed by the large boilered Atlantics, the first of which appeared five years later. Hitchin based Class C2, 4-4-2 No.3982 is seen on the turntable at Kings Cross Shed. The engine survived until 1935.

Large boiler Ivatt Class C1, 4-4-2 No.4434 was built in 1907 and was no doubt recorded by Arthur Mace at Kings Cross on the same occasion. Succeeded by the Pacifics on the East Coast Main Line it was withdrawn in 1945.

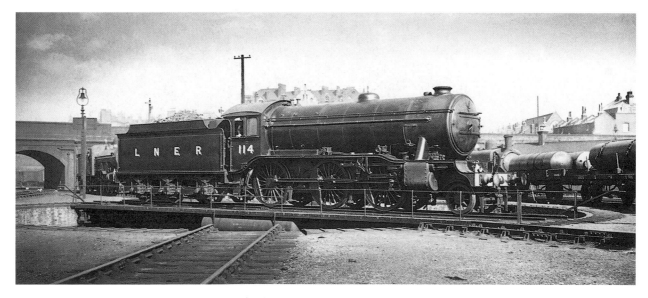

Gresley designed the powerful K3 Class 2-6-0s of which nearly two hundred were built between 1920 and 1937. They were superb mixed traffic engines and a worthy precursor to Gresley's later V2 2-6-2s. No.114, later B.R. No.61831, was built in 1924 and remained active until 1962.

Class A3, 4-6-2 No.2750 "Papyrus"..also at Kings Cross Shed was built in 1929 and bears the Scarborough Flyer headboard. This engine achieved fame in 1935 when it made high speed runs between Kings Cross and Newcastle in 3 hours 47½ minutes, so paving the way for the L.N.E.R.'s first streamlined express The Silver Jubilee later that year.

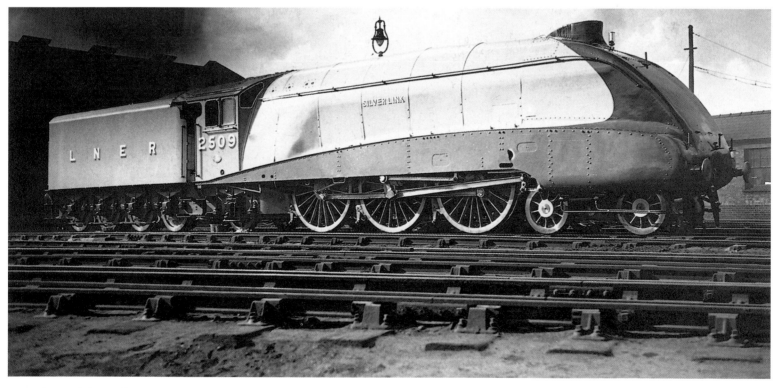

Another celebrated L.N.E.R. Pacific was A4 "Silver Link". During trial running of the Silver Jubilee in September 1935 this engine twice attained 112½ miles an hour and over a 10.6 mile stretch averaged 108.7 miles an hour.

The second of Gresley's Great Northern Railway built Pacifics was No.60102 "Sir Frederick Banbury". During its later years, it was transferred to the Great Central section and allocated to Leicester. It is seen here working the South Yorkshireman.

A rare wartime view of the same location - almost certainly near Rugby - with ex-Great Central Railway 4-6-0 No.5195 of Class B1 (later reclassified B18) piloting Class V2, 2-6-2 No.4820 with an ambulance train proceeded by three Southern Railway carriages. Wartime photography was severely restricted so one hopes that none of the occupants of the houses reported Arthur Mace's activities.

Years later in B.R. days, Class B1, 4-6-0 No.61131 heads a special train of L.M.R. stock. The location has altered little, but the all pervading B1's quickly decimated most of the older classes on the former Great Central section.

Over page
A grimy looking Peppercorn Class K1, 2-6-0 on freight duty in the North East.

Gorton based ex-G.C.R, Class C13, 4-4-2T No.6058, withdrawn in 1955 as B.R. No. 67403, heads a local passenger train out of Manchester London Road. A Class B3 4-6-0 waits with a later departure.

Great Northern stalwarts at Nottingham Victoria. On the far left is a K2 Class "Ragtimer" along with a pair of Ivatt J6 Class 0-6-0s.

Another K2 Class "Ragtimer" in the form of No.61773 based at Colwick Depot Nottingham, at the head of a Nottingham to Grantham train.

A Class B12/3, 4-6-0 heads a through train on the M.& G.N. joint line near Sheringham.

The gracefulness of the Great Central Atlantics is evident despite the advancing years as Class C4, 4-4-2 No.5360 heads an express south of Rugby along the Great Central Main Line. Built at Gorton in 1906, this engine survived until 1948. The ridge and furrow field alongside has survived since medieval times and is referred to in Sir John Betjeman's poem "The Great Central Railway".

The ridge and furrow formations are evident again in this war time scene at the same location featuring neglected Great Central section Pacific No.4471 "Sir Frederick Banbury" seen rather uncharacteristically at the head of a goods train.

Thompson O1 Class 2-8-0 No.63755 was one of five engines fitted with continuous vacuum brake and Westinghouse pumps to work iron ore trains from Tyne dock to Consett. The O1s were Thompson re-builds of Robinson's original Great Central 2-8-0s, This heavy drag of iron ore is being banked by an ex-North Eastern Railway Q7 0-8-0.

Over page
The rural character of the former Great Central Main Line is evidenced here as Thompson Class B1 4-6-0 No.61371 of Leicester 38C was recorded working hard on the Sheffield to Marylebone "Master Cutler" Express.

Class J25 0-6-0 No.5665 heads a mineral train through Barnard Castle. Forty of these engines were loaned to the G.W.R. in World War Two to compensate for the loss of Dean Goods 0-6-0s to the War Department. As L.N.E.R. No.1991 prior to the 1946 renumbering, this engine stayed on its home patch.

Ex-North British Railway Class D30, 4-4-0 No.62423 "Dugald Dalgetty" of Hawick heads a short freight. The engine appears to have a badly scorched smokebox door.

Although almost exclusively on the L.N.E.R. system, a few War Department Austerity 2-8-0s were allocated to the Great Western. Here, Shrewsbury based No. 90261 enters Leamington Spa on a down freight train. Notice the G.W.R. type top feed fitted to those engines working on W.R. lines.

In snow and so probably close to Arthur Mace's home at Rugby, Class O4/3, 2-8-0 No.3681 of Gorton heads a Great Central Line freight. These original Great Central engines were built between 1911/20 many for the Railway Operating Division during World War One. Under this guise the type saw widespread service overseas. Most were purchased back into L.N.E.R. stock in the 1920s. The type saw considerable re-building culminating in an almost complete transformation by Thompson, but many survived largely as built including the example shown here.

The Golden Years of British Steam Trains
SR

SOUTHERN RAILWAY

MILEPOST

INTRODUCTION

The Southern, though by far the smallest of the Big Four companies, was a dynamic railway with some of Britain's best loved trains: The Bournemouth Belle, The Devon Belle, The Brighton Belle and The Atlantic Coast Express. The principal constituents were the London and South Western, South Eastern and Chatham and London Brighton and South Coast; and territory ranged from the Kent coast to Cornwall.

The company's commitment to extensive electrification meant that the development of steam traction was limited. The railway had far less freight than the other companies and served hardly any coalfields with locomotive coal having to be brought in from afar. The many pre-grouping designs inherited by the Southern were of great antiquity and contrasted with the prolific work of it's two principal Chief Mechanical Engineers, R.E.L. Maunsell and O.V.S. Bulleid. Mausell's "Schools" were the most powerful British 4-4-0's and achieved legendary feats of haulage. The Southern was also distinctive in producing a revolutionary steam design during World War Two in the form of Bulleid's Pacifics which transformed the railway's express passenger services along with his Q1 Class 0-6-0s which brought to an end a 110 year long tradition of building inside cylinder 0-6-0s in Britain.

It is an interesting paradox that a railway so heavily electrified should retain so many antiquated steam designs and have the last main line to operate high speed steam expresses which survived on the London-Bournemouth and Weymouth route until 1967 – only one year before steam ended in Britain and almost twenty years after the Southern had ceased to exist. Some 1,845 Southern Railway locomotives embracing 90 different classes passed into British Railway's ownership in 1948.

A Wainwright Class C, 0-6-0 heads a down freight on Eynsford Viaduct.

Bulleid Merchant Navy Class 4-6-2 No. 35022 "Holland America Line" - in the short lived B.R. blue livery - spent some time in Rugby Testing Plant in December 1953/January 1954. No changes were made at the time, re-building commenced two years later.

Previous spread
The funeral train of Sir Winston Churchill on its way to Handborough (for Bladon and Blenheim) hauled by Battle of Britain Class 4-6-2 No. 34051 "Sir Winston Churchill" on 30th January 1965. The train consisted of Pullman Brake Car No.208, bogie luggage van No.S2464 (containing the coffin), Pulman Cars "Carina", "Lydia", "Perseus" and Pullman Brake Car "Isle of Thanet". Arthur Mace captures the solemnity of the occasion; the onlookers are not ordinary train spotters; there is an omnipresence about the characters which resembles a Munch painting.

Ashford based King Arthur Class 4-6-0 No.30802 "Sir Durnore" heads a local train to Ramsgate. Note the crossing keeper's cottage.

Schools Class 4-4-0 No.30918 "Hurstpierpoint" enters Ashford on a Charing Cross-Folkestone train, while a King Arthur Class 4-6-0 awaits the road with the Deal-Birkenhead train formed of W.R. stock.

It is Saturday and time to take the train to Canterbury for shopping and leisure pursuits. Class 2 MT, 2-6-2T No.41313 heads the train entering Aylsham.

Tunbridge Wells West with (left) an H Class 0-4-4T from Oxted, D1 Class 4-4-0 No.31470 approaching with a Tonbridge to Brighton train and an L Class 4-4-0 in the bay platform.

L Class 4-4-0 No.31769 approaches Orpington Station with a train for Dover via Ashford.

Passing Shortlands with a down continental express formed of the latest S.E.C.R. boat train stock about 1927 is King Arthur Class 4-6-0 No. E763 "Sir Bors de Ganis"

A chunky re-build of a Drummond 4-6-0, Class H15 No.E333 pauses at Axminster with a down Plymouth train.

Wainwright Class D, 4-4-0 No.1737 on a westbound train threads the white cliffs near the Warren Halt between Dover and Folkestone. The gentleman standing in the middle distance is presumably Arthur Mace's colleague and appears to have just photographed the train from a tripod.

Over page
Wainwright Class C, 0-6-0 No.31243 on shunting duties in the port of Dover. The ship is probably the "Isle of Thanet" of 1925, whose sister ship "Maid of Kent" was lost in World War Two.

King Arthur Class 4-6-0 No.30794 "Sir Ector de Maris" stands in the Night Ferry's traditional platform 2 at Victoria on a Kent Coast arrival.

Class I3, 4-4-2T No.2087 waits to depart from Victoria station on a Derby Day Pullman Race Special to Epsom Downs. In those pre-war days there would be several First Class race trains also steam hauled.

Another view of the former L.B.S.C. part of Victoria Station. A Brighton Works built L.M.R. Fairburn 2-6-4T has brought in an Oxted Line train forming the 3.8pm departure to East Grinstead.

During World War Two, with fears of possible invasion or aerial bombardment and a reduction in train services, many older engines were dispersed and placed in store away from depots. Possibly a unique photograph in view of the wartime veto on photography these three Stirling Class O1, 0-6-0's have been cleaned, their chimneys covered and fire irons removed. The two nearest, No's.1390 and 1093, were withdrawn in 1951.

Two Adams express locomotives of the mid 1890's await scrap at Eastleigh after the war. These 6' 6" 4-4-0s were T3 Class No.571 and X6 Class No.666. The former class is represented by No.563 in the National Railway Museum in York.

A line of withdrawn engines at Eastleigh in 1946. Leading is L.S.W.R. Jubilee Class A12, 0-4-2 No.555, L.B.S.C. Class D1 0-4-2T No. B633 and L.B.S.C. Class H1, 4-4-2 No.2040 "St Catherine's Point". They were towed away for scrap two years later.

Previous page
Wainwright Class E 4-4-0 No.31166 heads an up van train through Canterbury West. It was the last survivor of it's class being withdrawn in 1955.

Bulleid West Country Class Pacific No.34100 "Appledore" heads for London via Folkestone near Hawkesbury Street Junction. This once facinating area is now largely superseded by the Channel Tunnel. At right, behind the footbridge, the tracks lead into Dover Western Docks station recently closed.

Brighton-Cardiff through train near Lancing in the charge of West Country Class 4-6-2 No.34048 "Crediton" with G.W.R. carriages. The S.R. engine worked through to Salisbury.

The same location, West Country Class 4-6-2 No.34039 "Boscastle" heads the Brighton-Plymouth through train. Sets of pictures from the same location were a characteristic of Arthur Mace's work.

Drummond Greyhound Class T9, 4-4-0 No.310 pauses at Lewes with a Victoria-Eastbourne train prior to electrification in 1935. In S.R. days, several were fitted with six wheeled tenders to fit smaller turntables on ex-L.B.S.C.R. and S.E.C.R. lines.

A Brighton train enters Lewes from Eastbourne in the charge of an ex-L.B.S.C.R. Class B4, 4-4-0. Preparations for electrification in 1935 are in evidence.

It is blossom time in the Garden of England as Class D1 4-4-0 No.31735 heads a train over the S.E.R. route to the Kent coast via Ashford.

Previous page
A well known signal at the London end of Reading Station covering admittance to the former S.E.C.R. line at Reading South as well as the main line to Paddington.

King Arthur Class 4-6-0 No.30781 "Sir Aglovale" with an Ocean Liner express boat train from Victoria to Dover. Urie's L.S.W.R. Class N15 express passenger 4-6-0s with 6' 7" diameter wheels were incorporated into the King Arthur class by the S.R. More examples, with some modifications, appeared under Maunsell in 1925 and No 30781 is in this series. All examples had gone by 1962 but some of the names were inherited by the B.R. Standard 5 4-6-0s which partly superseded the King Arthurs, especially on the Waterloo, Bournemouth and Weymouth route so keeping the memory of these lovely engines alive until the end of S.R. steam in 1967.

Dramatic picture of an Ashford based Wainwright Class D, 4-4-0 on a Ramsgate-Victoria train. In pre-war days, a Pullman car was included on certain services on this route.

A busy scene at the Margate end of Ramsgate Station. Perhaps the coaling plant was out of order as engines are being coaled by crane on the right hand side. In the platform stands a Class D1 4-4-0 and at left a Class H 0-4-4T.

Between April and June 1948, two L.M.R. 2-6-4Ts, No's.42198/99, were loaned to the S.R. for trials, largely between Waterloo and Basingstoke and Victoria and Tunbridge Wells West. However, on 23rd and 24th April, No.42199 was tested between Victoria and Ashford via Maidstone East. It is seen leaving Ashford for London.

Two re-boilered Stirling Class R1, 0-6-0Ts, Nos.1337 and 1174, head an up continental express from Folkestone Harbour. A third 0-6-0T would be banking in the rear. At Folkestone Junction, a main line engine would take over. These elderly engines were replaced by surplus W.R. 0-6-0PT s in 1959 until electrification in 1961.

Battle of Britain Class 4-6-2 No.34066 "Spitfire" heads a down express on the Foord Viaduct at Folkestone. Beneath the viaduct is a Guy Arab IV of the East Kent Road Car Company.

Another view of the viaduct with a B.R. Class 5MT, 4-6-0 No.73087 on a down train.

An un-rebuilt Bulleid Battle of Britain Class 4-6-2 shuts off steam for a speed restriction while working a Victoria-Ramsgate train at Chestfield and Swalecliffe Halt, near Whitstable.

Re-built West Country Pacific No.34014 "Budleigh Salterton" on Foord Viaduct, Folkestone.

Again on the Foord Viaduct, Battle of Britain Class 4-6-2 No.34078 "222 Squadron". In the foreground is an East Kent Leyland PD1.

Stirling Class QI 0-4-4T No.A423 after its 1926 withdrawal was modified at Ashford Works for a stationary steam provision in which form it survived until 1933. This is surely one of Arthur Mace's most exciting pictures.

Previous spread
At Cannon Street, newly built Battle of Britain Class 4-6-2 No.21C167 "Tangmere" heads a down Dover express in the evening rush hour. This engine in un-rebuilt condition is undergoing restoration on the Mid Hants Railway.

The Erecting Shop at Eastleigh Works. Left and centre are two Class H15 4-6-0s, at right King Arthur Class 4-6-0 No.788 "Sir Urre of the Mount" still in wartime black livery.

Ashford Works Erecting Shop with Wainwright Class C, 0-6-0 No.1691.

A South Eastern and Chatham H Class 0-4-4T at Minster.

Canterbury West signal box with Classes H 0-4-4T and N 2-6-0 visible. The old Canterbury and Whitstable Railway engine shed can be seen in the background.

Class M7, 0-4-4T No.30047 heads a pull and push train to Brighton at Horsham Station, which was re-built in 1938 for the Mid-Sussex line electrification.

Schools Class No.30920 "Rugby" couples on to a boat train at Folkestone Junction.

South Eastern and Chatham Class D1, 4-4-0 No.31749 heads an up train at Sittingbourne Junction (for Sheerness).

The N Class Moguls were predominant in workings over the Reading-Redhill line. Here No.31411, one of the last batch to be built in 1933, heads a train through Gomshall and Shere.

Opposite
A Bulleid Battle of Britain Class Pacific nears the end of it's journey as it enters Birchington on Sea with a Victoria-Ramsgate express.

Previous spread
A D1 Class 4-4-0 with a lattice post London Chatham and Dover Railway signal.

Over page
A scene in the shed yard at Ramsgate with a Schools Class 4-4-0 taking coal. At right a Class H 0-4-4T and a Class T9 4-4-0 complete this pre-war view.

An interesting comparison of two railway's main line goods engines at Stewarts Lane shed Battersea. At left ex-S.E.C.R. Wainwright Class C, 0-6-0 No.31724 at right ex-L.B.S.C.R. Class C2x, 0-6-0 No. 32437. There was not a lot to choose between them but each railway's drivers preferred their own. In World War One, both companies introduced 2-6-0s for heavy freight work. Above, a King Arthur Class 4-6-0 heads a down express.

A party visit to Hither Green Shed with cameras focused on an N Class 2-6-0 as a C Class 0-6-0 simmers alongside.

Shed shunting in progress at Ramsgate Shed, with the engines in wartime black livery. At left re-boilered Stirling Class B1, 4-4-0 No.1452 (withdrawn in 1950), while a Class C, 0-6-0 shunts Class H, 0-4-4T No.1523. In the distance on the turntable stands a Class L1 4-4-0.

A pleasant scene on the S.E.R. main line in Kent with Ashford based King Arthur Class 4-6-0 No.30803 "Sir Harry le Fiselake".

Hard working re-built West Country Class 4-6-2 No.34034 "Honiton" passes Mitcheldever at speed with a down Ocean Liner Express to Southampton docks, the Pullman cars suggesting it was a Cunard working.

A Southern Railway rail built upper quadrant signal frames H Class 0-4-4T No.31519 propelling a pull and push train to Oxted.

Previous spread
Two Schools Class 4-4-0s run neck and neck between Hither Green and Grove Park. On the slow line No.900 "Eton" is working a Charing Cross-Dover train, while No.906 "Sherborne" heads a Cannon Street-Hastings Train on the fast line.

Over page
One of Bulleid's powerful wartime Austerity 0-6-0s of Class Q1, No.33004, shunts a covered wagon at the south end of Guildford Station.

An unidentified Drummond T9 Class 4-4-0 drifts down the 1 in 37 bank from Exeter Central to Exeter St David's on a Plymouth train.

Bulleid Battle of Britain Class 4-6-2 No.34084 "253 Squadron" heads a Victoria-Dover express past Minster Junction having taken the S.E.R. route via Ashford.

Opposite
Re-built Class D1, 4-4-0 No.31743 pauses at Canterbury East on a stopping train to Ramsgate via the S.E.R. route.

Two Southern Railways Schools Class 4-4-0s at Waterloo both on Portsmouth trains.

Schools Class 4-4-0 No.30928 'Stowe' is seen passing Paddock Wood with a Dover–Victoria express. The coal wagon and sidings for mixed freight eloquently remind us how the Railway provided an efficient co-ordinated transport system in those glorious pre-motorway days.